Safari

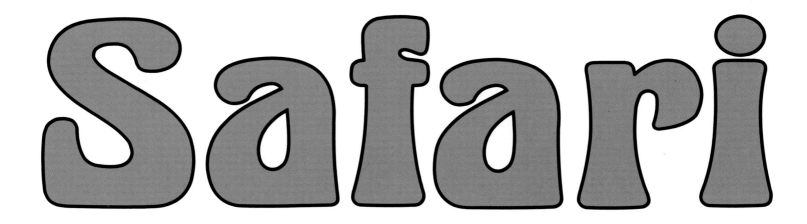

Safari

by Caren Barzelay Stelson
photographs by Kim A. Stelson

Carolrhoda Books, Inc./Minneapolis

LIBRARY OF CONGRESS CATALOGING-IN-PUBLICATION DATA

Stelson, Caren Barzelay.
   Safari / by Caren Barzelay Stelson.
      p.   cm. — (Carolrhoda photo books)
   Summary: Describes the animals, plants, and terrain that may be
observed while traveling on a safari through the Serengeti Plain of
Tanzania.
   ISBN 0-87614-324-9 (lib. bdg.)
   1. Zoology—Tanzania—Serengeti Plain—Juvenile literature.
[1. Zoology—Tanzania—Serengeti Plain. 2. Serengeti Plain
(Tanzania)] I. Title.
QL337.T3S74   1988
599.09678'27—dc19   88-1499
                                                           CIP
                                                            AC

Manufactured in the United States of America

1 2 3 4 5 6 7 8 9 10 98 97 96 95 94 93 92 91 90 89 88

*To our dear friend, Deb Eaton. We thank her for
her unabashed enthusiasm for this book.*

What do you imagine when you hear the word *Africa*? Do you think of jungles full of hanging vines? Do you picture snarling lions on the hunt? Do you see warriors hurling sharp spears? What do you imagine?

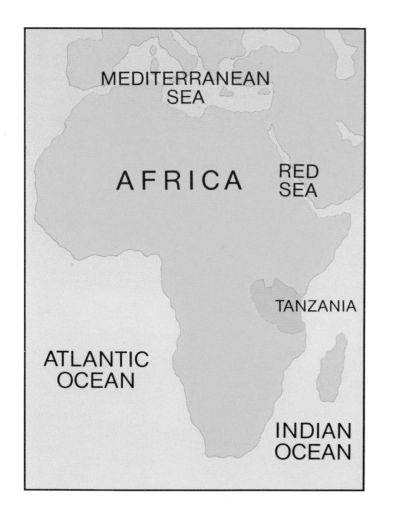

Let's take a journey to Tanzania. Tanzania is a country on the east coast of Africa, next to the Indian Ocean. It lies near the equator, where the temperatures are very high all year long. Let's take our cameras and go on a safari. So . . . roll up your sleeping bag, pack up your tent, and climb onto the safari truck.

The truck rumbles down a dirt road. The air is humid. The sun is blazing. As we put on our wide-brim hats, we think of our friends back home playing in the December snow. They are shivering, and we are getting sunburned.

The safari truck moves slowly westward. Gradually the air becomes dusty and dry. The ground turns sandy. Our guide tells us that we are traveling through countryside where the Masai tribe lives.

In the late afternoon, we stop to set up our campsite. To our surprise, we see some Masai boys coming to visit us. They are wrapped in reddish-brown blankets. Their curly hair is dyed the same color as their blankets. Large hoops dangle from their ears, and necklaces of beads and feathers hang around their necks. Although these African teenagers carry spears, they don't look fierce at all. The Masai boys begin to smile, and we smile back. Then they invite us to come to their *manyatta,* or village, in the morning.

The next morning our truck pulls up alongside a fence of tangled twigs. Within the fence are eight mounds of earth, each topped with animal hides and thatch. These mounds are Masai homes. Women and children look up from their chores. In minutes we are surrounded by curious villagers. As we get out of the truck, the women and children greet us. "*Jambo,*" they say as each raises the palm of one hand. It means "hello" in their language, Swahili. "*Jambo,*" we repeat.

12

One woman invites us into her home. She is very proud of this house, which she has built herself. We bend our heads to get through the door. It is dark and musty inside. The walls are made of dung, and the smell is strong. The small fire in the center of the main room fills the house with smoke. Two round windows the size of tennis balls let in a few rays of sunlight. This house has three rooms. One room is for sleeping, one is for cooking, one is for the young calves the Masai family owns. Calves are kept inside at night to keep them safe from prowling lions.

Our guide explains that cattle are very important to the Masai. They are used to trade for other goods. The more cattle a Masai man has, the richer he is. The cattle are used for food too, and can be given as gifts. A Masai recognizes each of his own cows. He can glance at his herd and know exactly which animals are there or missing. It is much like looking at a group of friends.

We recall others who live much like the Masai and realize how important these animals are to the people who herd them.

As we leave the *manyatta*, our truck bumps along two straight dirt tracks. We are heading for the Serengeti Plain—a large grassy area where thousands of wild animals live.

The Serengeti is now a national wildlife park, where animals can live without fear of being hunted by people. Everywhere we imagine lions ready to pounce. We look for hissing snakes and vultures waiting for the kill. We peer out the windows of our truck.

What a surprise! The grass is short and emerald green, as if it has been carefully mowed. And it has been. Thousands of grazers—zebras, impalas, cape buffalo, and wildebeests—have eaten their fill. They have left the eastern part of the Serengeti clipped and pruned. We don't have to hunt for any hidden animals. They are out in the open all around us. Zebras race alongside our truck. Giraffes run off at the sound of our motor, their long legs barely touching the ground. The colorful crowned cranes and the ugly vultures hardly notice us at all. Lizards blink, then scurry away into the cracks of rocks.

The Serengeti looks peaceful, until we see bones lying on the plain. A wildebeest has been killed and eaten by predators. Only its bones lie in a heap in the sunshine.

Now we try to see the Serengeti through the animals' eyes. It's a wild plain where each animal's goal is to survive. Who will eat? Who will be eaten? The herds of antelope now look nervous as they lift their heads to eye our truck. The zebras may play, but they also stop, turn, and smell the air for danger.

Our truck slowly rumbles on across the wild plain. Gradually the grass becomes tall and yellow. A few flies buzz in our ears. A few more tangle in our hair. Suddenly a swarm of flies fills the truck. Swatting the flies away, we see a large herd of wildebeests.

There must be a million flies traveling on the backs of these wildebeests. The wildebeest herd stretches to the horizon, just as the buffalo herds once covered the plains of North America.

We leave the wildebeests behind and begin the steep climb to Ngorongoro (n'GOR-oh-n'GOR-oh) Crater. This crater is known for the spectacular view from its rim, as well as for the animals that live on the floor below. Our guide tells us that this crater is home to more wild animals per square mile than anywhere else on earth.

From the mountaintop, it is a 2,000-foot drop to the bottom of the crater. The truck turns and heads down the mountain trail. Our shoulders smack against the sides of the truck as we go around sharp turns. We shut our eyes and hope we'll reach the crater floor in one piece.

Suddenly before us is a blue lake outlined in pink. As the truck moves closer, the pink band slowly turns into a flock of pink flamingos. Long-billed, long-legged flamingos glide through the water searching for food. Even the lake's beach is pink because flamingo feathers blanket the shore.

We look around us. Ngorongoro is a good name for this crater. In Swahili, Ngorongoro means "round, round." The crater walls completely surround us. The animals surround us too. We see herds of zebra, antelope, cape buffalo, and wildebeest.

A newborn zebra wobbles beside its mother. Tiny ostriches scurry to keep up with their parents. Young Thomson's gazelles stay close to the herd. The adult animals are watchful. They sniff the air for lions, cheetahs, and hyenas and nudge their babies closer to them.

We look for lions too, and find them. A lion pride, or family, sleeps in the afternoon sun. Like most lions, these seem to sleep 20 hours a day. Only one lion manages to lift his sleepy head as our truck passes. Others just roll over on their backs and yawn.

In the distance, dark gray forms stand quietly. Focusing our binoculars, we see a rhinoceros. The rhinoceros looks like a prehistoric animal. Weighing 2,000 pounds with large horns and thick skin, a rhino looks as if it could defend itself against just about anything. And it can—anything except people.

Rhinos are almost extinct. Hunting rhinos is illegal. But poachers, hunters who kill animals illegally, continue to kill rhinos for their horns. In some parts of the world, rhino horns are very valuable. We feel lucky to see this rhino alive.

We begin to understand the importance of wildlife parks. Their purpose is to keep the African wilderness a wild place. These parks may be the only chance Africa's wild animals have to survive.

The sky darkens as we settle down for the night in Ngorongoro Crater. Our tents are staked together. They make a tight circle around a blazing campfire. The circle of tents and the fire should keep the animals at a distance. Finally we fall asleep to the lively noises of the African night.

The early morning sun nudges us awake. It's time to wash up and head to Lake Manyara National Park. We soon find ourselves entering a jungle. Monkeys peer through the leaves. Pelicans line the tree branches.

As our truck rumbles along beside a stream, we are startled by the movement of large gray rocks in the water. Large snouts and pink eyes emerge. What we mistook for rocks are really hippopotamuses. Soon the splashing stops. The hippos settle together in a comfortable heap and sink back under the water. Our truck moves on just as the splashing and snorting begin all over again.

Lake Manyara is known for its elephants. Our guide stops the truck, and we watch for shadows in the bushes and listen for snapping branches. We are not disappointed. Three male elephants turn to hide in a clump of trees. One of the elephants looks as if he has a broken hip. The other male elephants walk slowly enough for their crippled friend to follow.

We spot a family of elephants grazing in a clearing. The female elephant is the family's leader, and she keeps a watchful guard over the herd.

A baby elephant stands close to its mother.

As the mother uses her trunk to pull up clumps of grass to eat, her baby tries to imitate her. It pulls up a few blades of grass at a time but doesn't always get them into its mouth.

When our guide starts the engine, the loud sound of the motor startles the elephants. The mother elephant looks at us and trumpets angrily. The other elephants gather around the baby, and all of them head into the jungle shadows.

On the way out of Lake Manyara Park, we stop at the huts of some research scientists. Lined up nearby are rows of bones. We see hippo, elephant, and rhino skulls. We learn that many of these animals were killed by poachers.

Poaching is a serious problem, explains one of the scientists, but another difficult problem also exists. Tanzania is a very poor country. Its population is growing rapidly, and more and more people must find land to

grow food for their families. The farmers see the wilderness as new land to farm. As people move farther into the wilderness, they compete for land with the animals that already live there. Animals need the land wild and open. People need the land tamed and fenced. These scientists and the Tanzanian government are trying to find ways to save the wilderness and to help the people.

Finally we head back to the campsite. It's time to pack up our tents, roll up our sleeping bags, and take off our wide-brim hats. Sitting back in the truck, we think of our Tanzanian safari. We have seen wild plains as well as jungles full of hanging vines. We know that lions sleep more than they snarl.

We have learned that a Masai boy may carry a spear but is often ready with a smile. We have begun to understand the problems of people and wild animals living together. Although our trip is over, we will never forget this African safari.